~A BINGO BOOK~

Greek & Roman Mythology Bingo

COMPLETE BINGO GAME IN A BOOK

Written by Rebecca Stark

ISBN 978-0-87386-424-4

Educational Books 'n' Bingo

Printed in the U.S.A.

GREEK & ROMAN MYTHOLOGY BINGO
Directions

INCLUDED:

List of Terms

Templates for Additional Terms and Clues

2 Clues per Term

30 Unique Bingo Cards

Markers

1. **Either cut apart the book or make copies of ALL the sheets. You might want to make an extra copy of the clue sheets to use for introduction and review. Keep the sheets in an envelope for easy reuse.**

2. Cut apart the call cards with terms and clues.

3. Pass out one bingo card per student. There are enough for a class of 30.

4. Pass out markers. You may cut apart the markers included in this book or use any other small items of your choice.

5. Decide whether or not you will require the entire card to be filled. Requiring the entire card to be filled provides a better review. However, if you have a short time to fill, you may prefer to have them do the just the border or some other format. Tell the class before you begin what is required.

6. There are 50 topics. Read the list before you begin. If there are any topics that have not been covered in class, you may want to read to the students the topic and clues before you begin.

7. There is a blank space in the middle of each card. You can instruct the students to use it as a free space or you can write in answers to cover topics not included. Of course, in this case you would create your own clues. (Templates provided.)

8. Shuffle the cards and place them in a pile. Two or three clues are provided for each topic. If you plan to play the game with the same group more than once, you might want to choose a different clue for each game. If not, you may choose to use more than one clue.

9. Be sure to keep the cards you have used for the present game in a separate pile. When a student calls, "Bingo," he or she will have to verify that the correct answers are on his or her card AND that the markers were placed in response to the proper questions. Pull out the cards that are on the student's card keeping them in the order they were used in the game. Read each clue as it was given and ask the student to identify the correct answer from his or her card.

10. If the student has the correct answers on the card AND has shown that they were marked in response to the *correct questions*, then that student is the winner and the game is over. If the student does not have the correct answers on the card OR he or she marked the answers in response to *the wrong questions*, then the game continues until there is a proper winner.

11. If you want to play again, reshuffle the cards and begin again.

Have fun!

TERMS

Achilles	Jupiter
Aphrodite	Mars
Apollo	Medusa
Arachne	Mercury
Ares	Minerva
Artemis	Minotaur
Atalanta	Mythology
Athena	Narcissus
Centaur(s)	Neptune
Cerberus	Olympian Gods
Cyclopses	Oracle
Demeter	Paris
Diana	Pegasus
Dionysus	Persephone
Echo	Perseus
Hades	Phaethon
Hephaestus	Pluto
Hera	Poseidon
Heracles	Prometheus
Hermes	Titan(s)
Hestia	Trojan Horse
Homer	Trojan War
Janus	Venus
Jason	Vulcan
Juno	Zeus

Note: Some of the names have alternate spellings not shown here.

Additional Terms

Choose as many Mythology terms as you would like and write them in the squares. Repeat each as desired. Cut out the squares and randomly distribute them to the class. Instruct the students to place the square on the center space of their card.

Clues for Additional Terms

Write two clues for each of your Mythology topics.

1. 2.	1. 2.
1. 2.	1. 2.
1. 2.	1. 2.

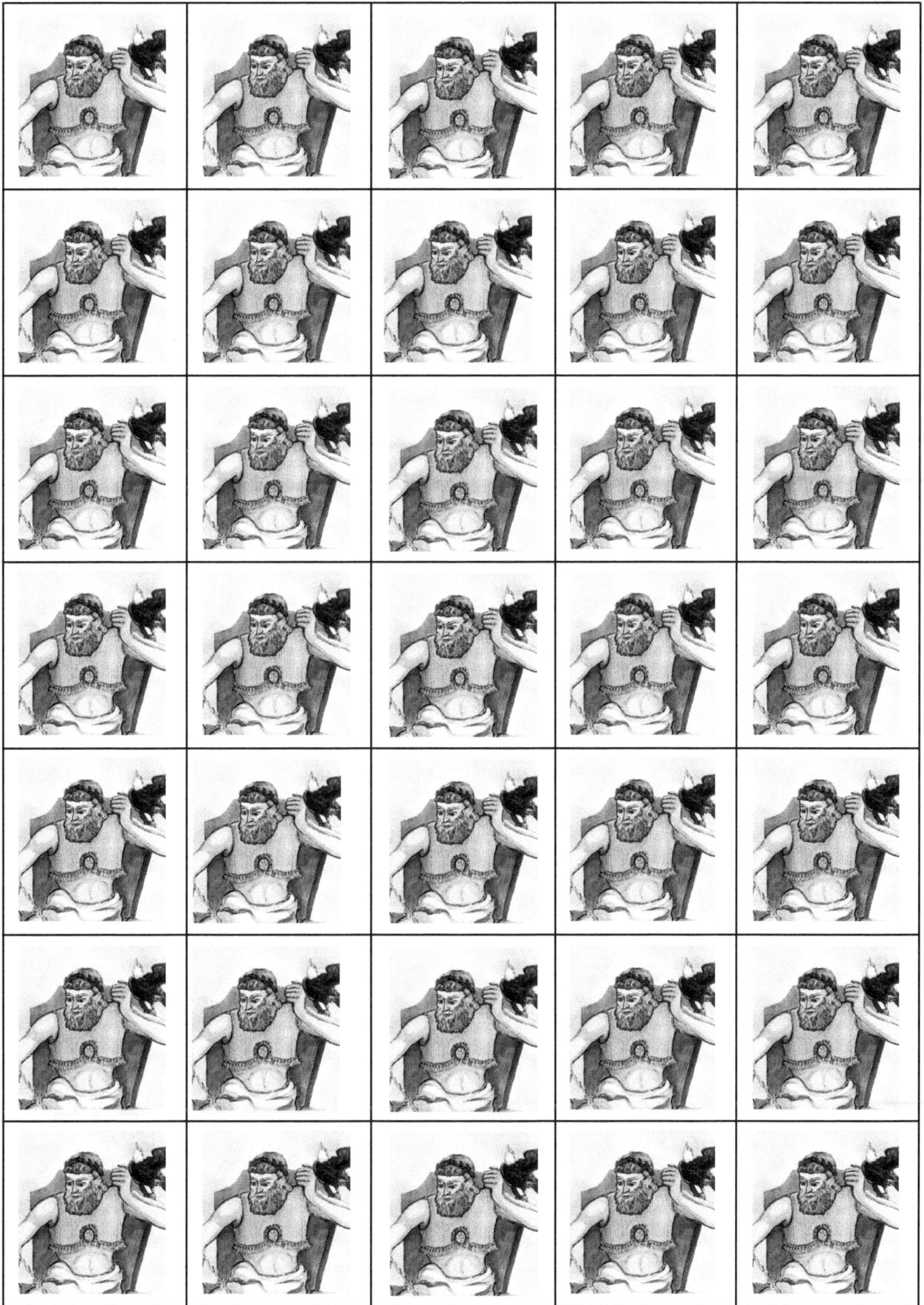

Achilles	**Aphrodite**
1. This Greek hero was the main character of Homer's *Iliad*. 2. The only vulnerable part of his body was his heel.	1. She was the Greek goddess of beauty and love. 2. This Greek goddess had a magic girdle (belt) that made men fall in love with her.
Apollo	**Arachne**
1. This Greek god was the son of Zeus and Leto and the twin sister of Artemis. 2. This Greek god of music and light played a golden lyre.	1. Athena turned ___ into a spider. 2. ___ angered Athena by challenging the goddess to a contest in weaving.
Ares	**Artemis**
1. In Greek mythology, ___ is the god of war. 2. This Greek god of war was not as popular with the Greeks as his counterpart, Mars, was with the Romans.	1. This Greek goddess of the hunt was associated with the moon. 2. She was the daughter of Zeus and Leto and the twin sister of Apollo.
Atalanta	**Athena**
1. It was prophesied that if she married, "she would lose herself." This was fulfilled when Zeus turned her into a lioness. 2. Her suitors had to race her. If the suitor won, she would marry him. If he lost, she would kill him.	1. She was the patron goddess of Athens. 2. This ancient Greek goddess was the goddess of wisdom, war and weaving. Her Roman equivalent was Minerva.
Centaur(s)	**Cerberus**
1. In Greek mythology they were creatures that were half man and half horse. 2. Chiron was the wisest ___ and the only one who was immortal. He gave up his immortality when Heracles accidentally wounded him.	1. ___ was the multi-headed dog that guarded the entrance to Hades. 2. The twelfth task of Heracles was to kidnap ___ from the Underworld.

© **Barbara M. Peller**

Cyclopses	**Demeter**
1. They were one-eyed giants in Greek (and later Roman) mythology.	1. This grain goddess of the ancient Greeks was known as Ceres by the ancient Romans
2. They gave Zeus his thunderbolt, Poseidon his trident and Hades his helmet of invisibility.	2. ___ 's daughter Persephone was abducted by Hades.
singular = *cyclops*	
Diana	**Dionysus**
1. She was the Roman goddess of the hunt.	1. This Greek god of wine was son of Zeus and Semele. He was the only Greek god to have a mortal parent.
2. Her Greek equivalent was Artemis.	2. This Greek god of wine had the power to drive a person mad. His Roman equivalent was Bacchus.
Echo	**Hades**
1. This nymph fell in love with Narcissus, but that love was unrequited.	1. It is the name of the Greek god of the dead and the Underworld. He is brother to Zeus and Poseidon.
2. As a punishment, Hera took away her voice so that she could only repeat the words of others.	2. His name is also used as the name for his domain, the land of the dead.
Hephaestus	**Hera**
1. He was the god of fire and metal working in Greek mythology.	1.This queen of the Greek gods was goddess of women and marriage.
2. He fashioned Zeus's aegis and scepter, the armor of Achilles, and Hera's throne.	2. She was the wife of Zeus. She was very jealous and often punished both gods and mortals who offended her.
Heracles	**Hermes**
1. He had to complete 12 tasks, or labors.	1. He was messenger of the Greek gods. His symbol was his caduceus, or staff.
2. Upon completing the tasks assigned to him by King Eurystheus, this hero gained immortality.	2. ___ had a helmet of invisibility and magic sandals that gave their wearer the ability to fly.

Hestia 1. She was the Greek goddess of the hearth fire. Her Roman equivalent was Vesta. 2. This Greek goddess tended the sacred fire in Olympus.	**Homer** 1. This Greek poet is believed to have lived in the eighth century BCE. 2. The Greek epic poems the *Iliad* and the *Odyssey* are attributed to this author.
Janus 1. He was the Roman god of gates and doorways and beginnings and endings. 2. This Roman god could see the past with one face and the future with the other.	**Jason** 1. This Greek hero was married to the sorceress Medea. He was the rightful king of Iolcos 2. He organized a group of heroes known as the Argonauts to go on a quest to find the Golden Fleece.
Juno 1. Women of Rome held a festival in her honor; it was called the Matronalia. 2. Her Greek equivalent was Hera. She was wife of Jupiter.	**Jupiter** 1. This god of the sky and thunder was the most important god in the Roman pantheon. 2. The symbol of this Roman god was the thunderbolt. He is also called Jove. His Greek equivalent was Zeus.
Mars 1. ___ was the Roman god of war. After Jupiter, he was the strongest and fiercest of the Roman gods. 2. Unlike Ares, his Greek counterpart, this Roman god of war was very popular and widely worshiped.	**Medusa** 1. She was one of the three Gorgons. Unlike her sisters, ___ was mortal. 2. Athena turned her hair into snakes and made her so ugly that anyone who looked at her eyes turned into stone.
Mercury 1. He was the Roman messenger of the gods. 2. The closest planet to the sun was named after this Roman god because it travels so quickly in its orbit.	**Minerva** 1. She was the Roman goddess of wisdom, warriors and crafts. 2. Her Greek equivalent was Athena.

Greek & Roman Mythology Bingo © **Barbara M. Peller**

Minotaur 1. Minos had Daedalus build a labyrinth in from which the ___ could not escape. 2. This creature terrorized Crete. It had the head and tail of a bull and the body of a man. The hero Theseus killed it.	**Mythology** 1. It is a body of stories that tell about the world view of a culture. 2. It is a collection of stories that tell about the gods, goddesses, demigods and heroes of a culture.
Narcissus 1. Some versions of the myth say that the goddess Nemesis punished him for spurning Echo. She made him fall in love with his own reflection. 2. His death led to the creation of a flower by the same name.	**Neptune** 1. This Roman god of the sea was brother of Jupiter and Pluto. Like Poseidon, his Greek counterpart, he was also worshiped as the god of horses. 2. The symbol of this Roman god was the trident.
Olympian Gods 1. These gods of ancient Greece ruled after the Titans were overthrown. 2. They include Zeus, Poseidon, Athena, Hera, Demeter, Ares, Apollo, Aphrodite, Hermes, Artemis, Hephaestus & Dionysus. (NOTE: Not all sources include Hephaestus and Dionysus and some include Hestia and Hades.)	**Oracle** 1. In ancient Greece it is where mortals went to hear phrophesies believed to be inspired by the gods. Priests and priestesses acted as intermediaries. 2. Apollo's ___ at Delphi was the most famous.
Paris 1. He was ordered by Zeus to decide which of three goddesses—Hera, Aphrodite, or Athena—should get the golden apple labeled "to the fairest." 2. His abduction of Helen led to the mythical Trojan War.	**Pegasus** 1. In Greek mythology ___ was a winged horse. 2. Bellerophon rode ___ to slay the monster known as the Chimera.
Persephone 1. She was Demeter's daughter and wife of Hades. Her Roman equivalent was Proserpina. 2. She had to stay with Hades part of the year because she had eaten some pomegranate seeds while in Hades. Greek & Roman Mythology Bingo	**Perseus** 1. King Acrisius set ___ adrift on the sea because of a prophecy that ___ would kill him. 2. This Greek hero fulfilled a prophecy by accidentally killing King Acrisius with a discus. © **Barbara M. Peller**

Phaethon 1. He begged his father Helios to let him drive the chariot of the sun. 2. When he lost control of the chariot of the sun, portions of earth were scorched.	**Pluto** 1. He was the Roman god of the Underworld. His Greek equivalent was Hades. 2. Originally this Roman god of the Underworld was considered the god of wealth because of the gold and other resources found in his realm.
Poseidon 1. In the mythology of the ancient Greeks, this Olympic god was god of the sea. He was also worshiped as the god of horses. 2. He was brother to Zeus and Hades. His Roman counterpart was Neptune.	**Prometheus** 1. This Titan created man out of clay and then gave him fire he had stolen from Zeus. 2. To punish man for accepting ___'s gift of fire, Zeus created Pandora, the first woman. Pandora opened the jar that released evils into the world.
Titan(s) 1. They were a race of powerful deities who were overthrown by the Olympians. 2. Cronus, a ___, was overthrown by his son Zeus. He was imprisoned in the part of the Underworld known as Tartarus like the other ___ who fought against Zeus.	**Trojan War** 1. This mythical was caused by Paris's abduction of Helen. For this reason it is said that Helen had the face that launched a thousand ships. 2. Most of the legends about the ___ come from Homer's works.
Trojan War 1. This mythical was caused by Paris's abduction of Helen. For this reason it is said that Helen had the face that launched a thousand ships. 2. Most of the legends about the ___ come from Homer's works.	**Venus** 1. She was the Roman goddess of love and beauty. Her Greek equivalent was Aphrodite. 2. She was mother of Cupid, the Roman god of love.
Vulcan 1. He was the Roman god of fire and volcanos. 2. He was known as the blacksmith god. His Greek equivalent was Hephaestus.	**Zeus** 1. He was supreme ruler of the Olympian Gods. Hera was his wife. 2. He overthrew his father, Cronus, who was ruler of the Titans.

Greek & Roman Mythology Bingo

© Barbara M. Peller

Greek & Roman Mythology Bingo

Janus	Hestia	Jason	Vulcan	Trojan Horse
Centaur(s)	Aphrodite	Venus	Minerva	Homer
Pluto	Paris		Juno	Neptune
Zeus	Achilles	Heracles	Poseidon	Jupiter
Mars	Cerberus	Demeter	Hera	Hermes

Greek & Roman Mythology Bingo

Zeus	Prometheus	Medusa	Oracle	Mars
Jupiter	Minerva	Atalanta	Achilles	Phaethon
Persephone	Cerberus		Diana	Heracles
Hephaestus	Perseus	Paris	Mythology	Homer
Hermes	Venus	Demeter	Centaur(s)	Hera

Greek & Roman Mythology Bingo

Zeus	Heracles	Minerva	Poseidon	Pluto
Cerberus	Aphrodite	Ares	Hestia	Minotaur
Achilles	Venus		Phaethon	Apollo
Paris	Persephone	Mars	Hephaestus	Medusa
Hera	Centaur(s)	Demeter	Mythology	Jason

Greek & Roman Mythology Bingo

Paris	Phaethon	Mars	Centaur(s)	Jason
Mercury	Atalanta	Hestia	Oracle	Pluto
Juno	Hephaestus		Trojan Horse	Vulcan
Heracles	Hades	Venus	Demeter	Ares
Echo	Hermes	Olympian Gods	Hera	Neptune

Greek & Roman Mythology Bingo

Hermes	Trojan Horse	Achilles	Atalanta	Centaur(s)
Mercury	Heracles	Ares	Diana	Aphrodite
Prometheus	Neptune		Dionysus	Cyclopses
Homer	Phaethon	Janus	Mythology	Echo
Minerva	Demeter	Pegasus	Paris	Juno

Greek & Roman Mythology Bingo

Apollo	Phaethon	Medusa	Prometheus	Neptune
Poseidon	Achilles	Echo	Hestia	Pluto
Oracle	Ares		Atalanta	Diana
Demeter	Mars	Mythology	Olympian Gods	Juno
Jupiter	Heracles	Janus	Pegasus	Jason

Greek & Roman Mythology Bingo

Janus	Phaethon	Cyclopses	Dionysus	Minerva
Jupiter	Jason	Cerberus	Aphrodite	Mercury
Medusa	Vulcan		Diana	Arachne
Paris	Hephaestus	Pluto	Zeus	Persephone
Demeter	Centaur(s)	Mythology	Olympian Gods	Apollo

Greek & Roman Mythology Bingo

Juno	Phaethon	Artemis	Poseidon	Arachne
Mercury	Prometheus	Oracle	Neptune	Atalanta
Pluto	Narcissus		Jason	Trojan Horse
Hera	Paris	Zeus	Echo	Hephaestus
Venus	Demeter	Olympian Gods	Achilles	Jupiter

Greek & Roman Mythology Bingo

Diana	Minerva	Cerberus	Pluto	Neptune
Echo	Prometheus	Juno	Achilles	Jason
Minotaur	Janus		Aphrodite	Artemis
Arachne	Hermes	Mars	Dionysus	Cyclopses
Hephaestus	Mythology	Ares	Zeus	Trojan Horse

Greek & Roman Mythology Bingo

Zeus	Poseidon	Atalanta	Oracle	Pegasus
Neptune	Arachne	Hestia	Aphrodite	Jason
Narcissus	Phaethon		Vulcan	Persephone
Mars	Homer	Echo	Mythology	Minotaur
Athena	Jupiter	Medusa	Hermes	Juno

Greek & Roman Mythology Bingo

Apollo	Phaethon	Achilles	Echo	Jupiter
Artemis	Minotaur	Dionysus	Diana	Hestia
Mercury	Prometheus		Medusa	Cerberus
Athena	Pluto	Mythology	Centaur(s)	Zeus
Ares	Demeter	Janus	Olympian Gods	Minerva

Greek & Roman Mythology Bingo

Minerva	Trojan Horse	Minotaur	Poseidon	Diana
Cerberus	Venus	Prometheus	Olympian Gods	Aphrodite
Janus	Cyclopses		Neptune	Oracle
Demeter	Hephaestus	Jason	Zeus	Mercury
Phaethon	Artemis	Narcissus	Ares	Arachne

Greek & Roman Mythology Bingo: Card No. 12

Greek & Roman Mythology Bingo

Athena	Trojan Horse	Apollo	Minotaur	Neptune
Prometheus	Artemis	Phaethon	Diana	Persephone
Poseidon	Atalanta		Cerberus	Cyclopses
Juno	Mythology	Arachne	Narcissus	Zeus
Demeter	Homer	Olympian Gods	Janus	Dionysus

Greek & Roman Mythology Bingo

Centaur(s)	Prometheus	Achilles	Diana	Athena
Arachne	Janus	Minotaur	Aphrodite	Phaethon
Echo	Vulcan		Medusa	Ares
Homer	Mythology	Narcissus	Atalanta	Apollo
Demeter	Oracle	Persephone	Jupiter	Juno

Greek & Roman Mythology Bingo

Dionysus	Diana	Achilles	Minerva	Poseidon
Apollo	Medusa	Hestia	Prometheus	Echo
Neptune	Janus		Pluto	Jason
Demeter	Minotaur	Artemis	Mythology	Athena
Jupiter	Hephaestus	Olympian Gods	Pegasus	Cerberus

Greek & Roman Mythology Bingo

Atalanta	Minotaur	Artemis	Pegasus	Perseus
Oracle	Persephone	Cyclopses	Mercury	Vulcan
Athena	Trojan Horse		Neptune	Cerberus
Paris	Arachne	Demeter	Dionysus	Zeus
Echo	Trojan War	Olympian Gods	Hephaestus	Phaethon

© Barbara M. Peller

Greek & Roman Mythology Bingo

Athena	Titan(s)	Hades	Minotaur	Centaur(s)
Dionysus	Echo	Mythology	Vulcan	Cyclopses
Diana	Zeus		Trojan War	Artemis
Hermes	Jupiter	Juno	Achilles	Persephone
Mars	Ares	Minerva	Poseidon	Trojan Horse

Greek & Roman Mythology Bingo

Jason	Narcissus	Arachne	Echo	Oracle
Phaethon	Athena	Mars	Neptune	Ares
Diana	Persephone		Hades	Pegasus
Hermes	Hestia	Mythology	Zeus	Medusa
Trojan War	Minotaur	Achilles	Titan(s)	Apollo

Greek & Roman Mythology Bingo

Neptune	Apollo	Minotaur	Artemis	Narcissus
Dionysus	Poseidon	Pegasus	Minerva	Vulcan
Titan(s)	Centaur(s)		Aphrodite	Jason
Medusa	Trojan War	Mars	Hephaestus	Hades
Pluto	Perseus	Jupiter	Juno	Olympian Gods

Greek & Roman Mythology Bingo: Card No. 19

Greek & Roman Mythology Bingo

Narcissus	Titan(s)	Poseidon	Minotaur	Aphrodite
Atalanta	Cerberus	Mercury	Mars	Oracle
Trojan Horse	Cyclopses		Paris	Hestia
Hermes	Juno	Hera	Hephaestus	Trojan War
Heracles	Venus	Perseus	Zeus	Hades

Greek & Roman Mythology Bingo

Dionysus	Apollo	Mercury	Minotaur	Homer
Trojan Horse	Hades	Arachne	Artemis	Janus
Persephone	Jupiter		Titan(s)	Achilles
Mars	Minerva	Trojan War	Hermes	Juno
Paris	Perseus	Olympian Gods	Athena	Hephaestus

Greek & Roman Mythology Bingo

Pluto	Medusa	Hades	Prometheus	Athena
Oracle	Poseidon	Jason	Artemis	Aphrodite
Arachne	Vulcan		Janus	Cyclopses
Trojan War	Hermes	Hephaestus	Hestia	Centaur(s)
Perseus	Ares	Titan(s)	Persephone	Mercury

Greek & Roman Mythology Bingo

Atalanta	Titan(s)	Minerva	Prometheus	Olympian Gods
Apollo	Narcissus	Jupiter	Dionysus	Hestia
Medusa	Athena		Hera	Janus
Persephone	Perseus	Trojan War	Ares	Hephaestus
Homer	Juno	Venus	Mars	Hades

Greek & Roman Mythology Bingo: Card No. 23

Greek & Roman Mythology Bingo

Atalanta	Narcissus	Centaur(s)	Titan(s)	Artemis
Neptune	Olympian Gods	Mercury	Oracle	Janus
Cyclopses	Pegasus		Athena	Persephone
Homer	Hera	Trojan War	Ares	Trojan Horse
Heracles	Paris	Perseus	Poseidon	Venus

Greek & Roman Mythology Bingo

Paris	Mercury	Titan(s)	Achilles	Hades
Hestia	Homer	Dionysus	Atalanta	Aphrodite
Trojan Horse	Artemis		Hera	Trojan War
Pegasus	Hermes	Venus	Perseus	Vulcan
Olympian Gods	Centaur(s)	Arachne	Echo	Heracles

Greek & Roman Mythology Bingo

Hades	Titan(s)	Hera	Oracle	Pegasus
Mars	Poseidon	Artemis	Narcissus	Atalanta
Homer	Medusa		Vulcan	Paris
Athena	Prometheus	Hermes	Perseus	Trojan War
Cyclopses	Echo	Achilles	Venus	Heracles

© Barbara M. Peller

Greek & Roman Mythology Bingo

Hera	Arachne	Titan(s)	Narcissus	Cerberus
Homer	Medusa	Dionysus	Trojan War	Aphrodite
Mythology	Venus		Perseus	Paris
Pegasus	Apollo	Mercury	Heracles	Hestia
Athena	Vulcan	Hades	Pluto	Cyclopses

Greek & Roman Mythology Bingo

Neptune	Narcissus	Zeus	Titan(s)	Arachne
Cerberus	Hades	Hera	Mars	Vulcan
Venus	Persephone		Pegasus	Oracle
Cyclopses	Pluto	Jupiter	Perseus	Trojan War
Prometheus	Diana	Athena	Heracles	Homer

Greek & Roman Mythology Bingo

Hades	Narcissus	Pegasus	Dionysus	Diana
Homer	Mars	Mercury	Cyclopses	Pluto
Trojan Horse	Hera		Aphrodite	Titan(s)
Cerberus	Hermes	Jason	Perseus	Trojan War
Atalanta	Artemis	Heracles	Apollo	Venus

Greek & Roman Mythology Bingo

Centaur(s)	Titan(s)	Oracle	Diana	Trojan War
Hestia	Pegasus	Medusa	Vulcan	Aphrodite
Heracles	Ares		Cyclopses	Mercury
Homer	Apollo	Narcissus	Perseus	Hera
Hermes	Minerva	Venus	Hades	Jason

　　　　　　© **Barbara M. Peller**

www.ingramcontent.com/pod-product-compliance
Lightning Source LLC
LaVergne TN
LVHW061337060426
835511LV00014B/1976